WAR HEROES

—A MURDER MYSTERY—

Sixth Book in the Zuma Mystery Series

JEROME RABOW, PH.D.

ISBN 978-1-955156-72-1 (paperback)
ISBN 978-1-955156-73-8 (digital)

Copyright © 2021 by Jerome Rabow, Ph.D.

All rights reserved. No part of this publication may be reproduced, distributed, or transmitted in any form or by any means, including photocopying, recording, or other electronic or mechanical methods without the prior written permission of the publisher. For permission requests, solicit the publisher via the address below.

Rushmore Press LLC
1 800 460 9188
www.rushmorepress.com

Printed in the United States of America

TABLE OF CONTENTS

Chapter 1: A Botched Robbery........................5
Chapter 2: A Triple Murder 8
Chapter 3: Why are You Quiet?....................13
Chapter 4: Blame It on the Sun 15
Chapter 5: Dust Yourself Off 18
Chapter 6: A Successful Visit 22
Chapter 7: Why Are You Afraid of the Truth?.............26
Chapter 8: A Successful Robbery 28
Chapter 9: A Farewell............................29
Chapter 10: Clues................................31
Chapter 11: A Booking............................34
Chapter 12: Where Have All the Flowers Gone?.............38
Chapter 13: Another Bank 41
Chapter 14: Buddies..............................43
Chapter 15: All Decent Chaps 45
Chapter 16: The Student Reminds the Mentor.............47
Chapter 17: An innocent Helps 49
Chapter 18: Another Alpha........................51
Chapter 19: Working with the Enemy 53
Chapter 20: Cooperation Doesn't Pay...............55
Chapter 21: Going back 58
Chapter 22: The Trial............................61

CHAPTER 1

A Botched Robbery

Detective Joe Zuma received the call at 10:05 and by 10:17, he and his associate arrived at the bank to see four young men lying on the ground. He laughed out loud upon arriving at the bank where this botched bank robbery by the four males, two black and two Latinos, had taken place. He never laughed at suspects unless they had spoken so this was unusual behavior that his colleague Pat Vasquez noticed. Zuma did not reflect on his laughter. For him, it just looked funny. The security guard proudly described to Zuma that the four of them were very nervous when they showed up at the bank's door and could barely handle their guns.

"If I opened the door for them and let them go first, I would be able to press the alarm button which is outside, then silent, and that would take less than fifteen minutes for you guys to show up. Man, were those kids surprised."

Zuma leaned down and spoke.

> "What's the matter with you kids?
> Have you all lost that lovin' feelin'?"

He began singing the words.

> "You're trying hard not to show it
> But baby I know it.
> You've lost that lovin' feeling."

The four young men and Pat Vasquez stared at Zuma as if he was from another planet. They had no idea what he was doing, and Pat was also unsure. He had often heard Zuma sing songs appropriate to a situation but never to suspects. He decided not to say anything about the laugh or the singing.

The young men were taken to Zuma's precinct. He grilled them trying to find out what they needed money for, who put them up to it, and what they were going to do with the money. They say the idea came from something they saw on TV and it looked easy. They enjoyed buying the guns and practicing at a firing range. His conclusion was that these were innocent, naive kids. They had no records. He tells them he is not even going to book them but asks if they have ever seen the rain, and before they can answer he starts singing again:

> "There's a calm before the storm.
> I know it's been coming for some time.
> When it's over so they say
> It'll rain a sunny day.
> I wanna know have you ever seen the rain?"

"Boss, I think we can let the kids go."

"Sure, Pat. I'm happy to let them go. It's nice to see young people who can get along even for a botched robbery. Maybe they know the famous *I Have a Dream* speech. Do you know it, kids?"

The boys were speechless and stared at each other, shook their heads no, and left as Pat gave them a nod to leave.

"Boss, what do you think you were doing with the laughing, the singing, and the reference to Martin Luther King Jr.'s speech?"

"Just trying to educate Pat, just trying to educate."

Pat Vasquez knew something was off with his boss. He had worked with Zuma for ten years and seen him pursue all kinds of criminals with diligence and respect. He had tremendous respect for Zuma's intelligence and judgments. He had sung to Pat many times songs that captured the real situations they were encountering but he had never sung to suspects. He was at loss as to what to say but thought he had better discuss it with Claudia, Zuma's wife. He had an honest and open relationship with her, and she would trust his observations. She might be able to confirm this unusual behavior and together, they might be able to come up with a plan.

CHAPTER 2

A Triple Murder

A few days after the four boys are released, a phone call came into the Santa Monica precinct about a shooting on the third street mall. When Zuma and Pat show up, they see two of the bodies who have been shot to death were part of the group that had been set free. They were both Latinos. The third person lying on the ground is a young woman. She is conscious. Zuma is aghast. He is speechless and is staring at the corpses. Pat had never seen his boss so upset about the murders that he was not able to respond. Zuma is standing as if he was frozen at the two young Latino boys. Pat is now convinced that something is definitely going on with his boss. Zuma has never been one not to act. He decides to act.

"Boss, I'll call an ambulance for the girl. What are you thinking? You seem upset and shook up."

"I'm thinking, Pat, that two of these dead kids are my responsibility. If I had booked them or locked them up and made their parents come down, maybe they would not just be hanging around the mall looking for trouble thinking that nothing bad had happened to them. If I had brought their parents in, maybe the kids would have been grounded and not even been here."

"Boss, that's an awful lot of 'ifs'. And it doesn't explain why they were shot, who shot them, and who this third person is and if she had anything do with the kids."

"Pat, I know you're right about my speculations and what we should be focused on, but my brain keeps doing this thing that it never did before."

"Boss, I can finish up here. I'll rope off the area and not let folks go home till we had a chance to ask them about the shootings. I'll get the bodies down to the morgue and will ride with the ambulance to the hospital. Once all fingerprints are run, I'll call the parents. You just head home. There'll be a full report on your desk when you show up tomorrow."

Zuma thought the young woman was beautiful. She had golden-brown skin that looked as smooth as melted ice cream, black curly hair, long legs covered by blue jeans, and an ample bosom. She'd be a catch for anyone he thought.

"Young lady, please give me your name and a number so I can call your family. When we get to the hospital, I'm going to ask you some questions. Maybe your family can meet us. My colleague Pat Vasquez will accompany you in the ambulance."

"I'm Aliya Johnson. I want to make the phone call to my parents."

Zuma noted that despite the bullet wound, how strongly the young woman acted.

"Mom? Dad? I've been in an accident but I'm fine. They are taking me to Saint John's for X-rays to make sure. Yes, don't worry, I really am okay."

"Boss, she's still in the X-ray lab and the gal's parents just arrived. I won't say much to them until the results of the lab are out. I'll finish up here. Would you like me to come over later? I think Claudia should be told what is going on and I'd like to be there."

"Thanks, Pat. Let's meet for dinner. I can grab a nap before we meet."

Joe Zuma had rarely taken or felt a desire to take naps. In the past month or so, he had a desire to do so but got rid of the feeling by taking a cup of coffee. As he headed home for his nap, the words to a song began playing in his head.

> "Hello darkness, my old friend
> I've come to talk with you again."

He had always loved "The Sounds of Silence" by Simon and Garfunkel. He knew the words conveyed an image of darkness and feelings of sadness and loneliness, but he had never thought it applied to him. He just loved the music and words. The last words, right before he nodded off and lost awareness, also came from the song.

> "A vision softly creeping
> Left its seeds while I was sleeping.
> And the vision that was planted in my brain
> Still remains."

In the meeting with the girl and her parents, Pat found out that Aliya Johnson was nineteen-year-old and a graduate of Santa Monica High School. Her father was black, and the mother was white.

"Mr. and Mrs. Johnson, your daughter is most fortunate. The bullets came from one angle so there was probably only one shooter. There were two slugs in each of the two males. The shooter was an excellent marksman as both bullets entered the sides of their head."

"Our daughter has been trained to drop to the ground the moment she hears anything that sounds like a shot. That's something we are taught in the Marines. We thought it advisable that she learn to do this even though it is not Iraq or Afghanistan."

"The doctor will still want to keep her overnight to make sure there is no trauma. The dead boys, Anthony Perez and Hector Sanchez, went to Catholic High School, were seniors, and both 18. One of the other officers who was detaining the public spoke and said the two of the people were pretty sure they saw the shooting. They were antsy about saying anything anymore. I'll speak with them later. They are being detained right now."

"Do you know the two boys who were shot?"

"Why should we talk to you, officer?"

"It might help us solve this murder."

"Every time a black person helps the cops solve a murder, he always gets his ass in trouble. Please go solve your murder and find out who shot our daughter. They must have been pros. Our daughter is my alpha child. We trained her well. I hope you are trained as well."

"In case you change your mind, here's my card."

"I understand why minorities were hesitant to cooperate with the police, Joe, but when your own daughter has been shot, I wonder if there is something beyond refusal to cooperate. I think it might be fear and what the fear could be about. I have enough time before meeting with you and Claudia and I want to head back to the mall where the young man and girl had been detained. Maybe I can find something more about the shootings."

"I realize you are probably scared about saying anything, but I guarantee your names will never be revealed. I promise you."

"Sarah, you go first."

"Ok, Allan, I will."

The young boy and girl now seemed to be a couple.

"We were walking about twenty yards behind the three people and this person walked rapidly past the two of us. We noticed and I said to Allan it's amazing how fast he is walking. I stopped in my tracks when I heard these loud pops. Sounded like balloons bursting?"

"Sarah thinks it was a white male. I thought it could be a mannish Latino female. When I heard these loud noises, I thought it might be guns and I told Sarah to get down. As we dropped to the ground, I see the three of them on the ground while the person who passed us is now running."

Pat realizes that the information is completely worthless. In the courtroom, testifying that they had different opinions about the racial and gender identities of the shooters would be the kind of testimony that would be of no value.

"Thank you for your help. I'll take your names but will protect you by not letting anyone know you spoke with me. Here is my card in case you think of anything else that might be helpful to us. You are welcome to go home now. I know we've kept you and I can have Officer Elliott drop you off at your homes.

"Thank you for your offer. We live together and we're only two blocks away. Sarah, do you want to ride or walk?

"Let's walk, Allan. It will calm me down."

CHAPTER 3

Why are You Quiet?

Zuma, Claudia, and Pat met at the Shangri-La. This was their favorite place for dining. After drinks had been ordered, Pat began:

"Boss, I would never speak behind your back but what I wanted to say to you, I wanted Claudia to also hear. I would like her to know what I see and maybe she sees the same thing. If she doesn't, I'll just not worry or be concerned."

"Shoot, Pat. I trust your judgment and opinions."

"For the past few weeks, I noticed you have not been talking much to me. You seem to get lost in your thoughts. Sometimes, I hear you humming songs to yourself. The song thing is what you usually do with me. This morning, when you did it with suspects, I became worried, and when you questioned them about the King speech, I was convinced that something was going on with you. Your laughing at them while they were lying on the floor was very inappropriate. Without any idea of what is going on with you, I am concerned and that is why I wanted to speak with you and with Claudia present."

Zuma started to respond but saw that Claudia wanted to speak.

"Thank you, Pat, for coming to us. I have also noticed some things but could not be sure if it was just a response to some extra stress at work. Joe, darling, you have become less communicative, more removed, and less attentive to me and seem to forget things I have told you. Is something going on that you have been unable to talk about?'

"The only thing I've noticed that is different is my getting sleepy in the afternoon and the coffee doesn't seem to help. That both of you see something similar is shocking to me. I was unaware that I was doing these other things. And Pat, you are right. Why the hell would I sing to suspects, laugh at boys lying on the ground, or quiz them?"

"Joe, would you be willing to call the therapist who helped you once before?"

"Yes, I will. Thank you both for letting me know what was upsetting you. I don't want what I'm doing to scare either of you or to interfere with my work. I'll call tonight after dinner and make an appointment with her as soon as she is able to see me. Let's order now. I promise not to be quiet or to sing to myself."

CHAPTER 4

Blame It on the Sun

When Zuma and Pat arrived at work, the coroner's report confirmed the identities of the two victims. He also found that the two males had no records, but the female had been arrested as a suspect in an armed robbery one year ago along with two males. The males were convicted. They had not worn masks and were easily identified on a security tape. The woman was the supposed driver but was let go when no evidence or witnesses could be found.

"Pat. We've got three families to visit. I'd like it if we can do them together. Let's do the victims' families first."

The Perez family lived in an expensive two-story, Victorian house just south of San Vicente on 24 street. It was painted light grey and had dark trim. Both detectives looked at each other in admiration that this Latino family lived in this expensive house in an expensive part of town. When they were let in, they were introduced to another couple that turned to be the parents of Hector Sanchez.

"Mr. and Mrs. Perez and Mr. and Mrs. Sanchez, we are very sorry about the loss of your sons. Do you think, even though this has got to be a difficult time for all of you, that you could say something about their relationship to each other or to the girl who was also shot?"

Mrs. Perez spoke first.

"The boys were very close. We live just two blocks away from each other and they both attended Franklin Elementary School together. They did pretty much everything together: homework, sports, surfing, rollerblading. We all come from poor backgrounds but have done well in America and all four of us agreed we did not want our children to be deprived. We moved here because we knew they would get a better education. When they asked for surfboards or roller skates, we were happy to buy them. We did not want them to feel they didn't belong and couldn't do things with the other richer kids. When they were ready to start high school, we thought it would be better for them to be in a more structured and disciplined environment. All of us still work and we did not want them to have a lot of unsupervised time, so we decided to send them to Catholic school. We knew we had spoiled them but were sure the nuns and the priest would put them in their place and teach them that they were privileged but not entitled to anything."

Mr. Sanchez chimed in.

"The day the two of them brought that girl into my home, I knew there would be trouble. She was from a poor family and I knew she could manipulate our innocent boys. She was only a year older, but you knew she had been around and had a lot more experience and could easily recognize how naïve our sons were."

"Mr. Sanchez, or any of you, could you be more specific as to what you saw or heard from Aliya Johnson?"

"I overheard her speaking once about how Latinos were favored more than blacks and how Latinos had turned on blacks whom they felt had not worked as hard as they had."

"She even argued with me once saying that if our sons robbed a bank, they would probably get off easily because of our money and where we lived while if she robbed a bank, she would be treated more harshly." These last words were spoken by Mr. Perez.

"Did either of you speak to your sons about your concerns?"

"Whenever we did it with all six of us, they laughed and said she talks big but doesn't do anything bad. They said she was lots of fun, liked to dance and go to movies. They also said they were ok with paying for her whenever the three of them went out because she knew the places to go."

"Do you each have other children?"

"Yes, we each have two daughters, three years younger than our sons. The four of them are just like the two boys were. They do everything together."

"Again, we are sorry for your loss. If you can think of anything else you could tell us that might explain who would want your boys shot or anything about Aliya Johnson that you have not told us, please give Detective Vasquez or me a call. Here are our cards."

"No one would want to shoot our boys. It was probably that damn angry black girl that someone wanted dead. I'm sure she upset a lot of people with her anger."

"What do you think, Pat?"

"Same old story, Boss. Poor people making it, then turning on people who haven't made it and blaming them for their pain or loss."

"Your right, Pat, but sometimes the blame can be accurate."

Zuma started to hum right after his toothpick came out. Pat smiled and knew that this routine of a toothpick and humming was what his boss did when he was thinking about the situation.

He didn't recognize the tune and asked.

"It's a Stevie Wonder song but I like the Diana Ross version. The words are more fitting to what you described, Pat, when people seek to blame someone or something and can't see where the blame belongs."

> "I'll blame it on the sun,
> The sun that didn't shine,
> I'll blame it on the wind and the trees."

Pat smiled and wondered if Zuma had already seen the therapist that he promised he would call.

CHAPTER 5

Dust Yourself Off

The apartment where Aliya Johnson's parents lived was a one-bedroom located on Pico at 26th street. It was a noisy street with cars coming off and getting ready to enter the 10 freeway. Because the apartment was on the first floor, it was very noisy. All the apartments had bars on the windows. Zuma could read the 'Semper Fie" sign and saw the picture of a purple heart on the windows behind the bars.

"Mr. and Mrs. Johnson, Detective Vasquez has told me you do not wish to answer any questions. We are very sorry for your loss. We would very much like you to reconsider and talk with us now. If this is not a good time, we can come back later."

A truck roared past the apartment and Mr. Johnson waited for the noise to subside. Zuma noticed the separate photographs of the Johnsons in their dark blue official Marine dress outfits. They looked proud. There was another photograph of what must have been their daughter in a ballet outfit. She must have been about five. The apartment was very neat. Zuma's eyes fell upon the high degree of shine on Mr. Johnson's shoes. The Johnsons, he thought, have continued their Marine training for neatness and cleanliness.

"Do you expect me to believe that you're interested in finding out who tried to murder our daughter? I'm sure she is for you another black girl, a statistic. The article in the paper gave five times as much space to those poor Latino boys compared to what they gave to our child. Our daughter got the one line about her being a graduate of Santa Monica High School and that she survived. We've made progress in this country, Detective. Years ago, when a black girl was murdered, there might not even be one line. More likely, there would be no mention at all. Our leaders like Martin Luther King, Jr. get all the attention but poor blacks who get shot are still ignored. Ignored like my daughter was ignored. Excuse me, I don't want to be accused of being dramatic. She only got one goddamn line."

Those words along with the high shine from Mr. Johnson's shoes and the purple heart medal that he wore on his white shirt made a deep impression upon Zuma. He knew he would not forget it. He regretted that this man who had risked his life for his country and had been wounded was being treated so badly after his service and sacrifice.

"Mr. and Mrs. Johnson, Detective Vasquez and I promise to do everything we can to find out who tried to kill your daughter. But we can also use your help if you are willing."

"My husband and I have heard promises like that before. Solomon may not want to say a thing, but I will talk with you because I believe your desire to find out who killed the boys might lead you to the person who shot Aliya. Detective, Aliya was a strong-willed woman. Growing up in a bi-racial family but being light-skinned allowed her to move between two different worlds if she wanted. She chose to identify with Solomon's world, the black community, more than mine. I had no problem with that. I knew she would have it easier if she tried to stay in the white world, but she loved her dad and wanted to identify with him more than me."

"Thank you, Mrs. Johnson. Can you tell us more about her interests? Was she working after she graduated?"

"Our daughter always wanted to be a performer. She took dance lessons in school. I think a few of the instructors saw talent and encouraged her to learn to play the piano. Lady Gaga was her idol. She wanted to be like her because Lady Gaga had made changes in the way people looked at dancers or listened to music. She always had trouble keeping a job. All of them were low-level entry jobs and she got bored too easily."

"Did you support her financially?"

"Oh no. Solomon and I knew that a woman who identified as being black had to learn to support herself. We named her Aliya because it means 'Dust yourself off and try again.' In Hebrew, it means ascend. Our daughter always wanted to ascend. She figured out a way to do it by giving a piano lesson to younger kids from upscale families north of Montana Avenue, right here in Santa Monica. She rode her bike to their homes and was really good with children. She is a very ambitious child."

"So, Aliya would teach kids during the day and she would go out in the evenings? Is that correct, Mrs. Johnson?"

"Yes, she would never want to miss an opportunity to dance. She told me that some of the clubs would let her in for nothing because her dancing would become an attraction for the other dancers."

"Did you know the two boys who were also shot?"

"I never met them. Sometimes, they would come and pick her up. She said they were spoiled rich Latinos who were naïve. They were willing to pay for her way into the club and for drinks. Aliya said she was educating them about Los Angeles."

"Did your daughter ever talk about her future and what she wanted to do?"

"That's interesting that you ask. It was only in the past few months that she mentioned a future. She wanted to go back east and register in a program that had a very good reputation for developing artists who could sing, dance, and play an instrument. She said it was a lot of money, but she was hoping to get a scholarship. She had started singing lessons with someone that one of her high school teachers recommended. She was paying for that on her own."

"It definitely sounds like your daughter is a very ambitious person. Is there anyone you know who might want to hurt her?"

"Our daughter had strong opinions and we always encouraged her to express them, Detective. I don't know if she said anything at the place she worked at or at the homes of the children she tutored. Or even at the clubs she danced in. But she was an outspoken human being. No one who met Aliya would forget her."

"Thank you for your help, Mrs. Johnson. I believe the information you provided to us will be most helpful. I'd appreciate it if you can tell us your first name."

"It's Adar. It stands for fire."

"Can you also give us a list of the places she worked at and the names of the homes she tutored in?"

"I can't help you with that, Detective. We picked up her phone at the coroner's. We haven't touched it. If you trace the numbers she called, you might find out the information you requested. I'm happy to give you her phone. Please return it when you have finished. It's expensive and we would like to hold on to it."

"What do you think, Pat?"

"Their daughter's speaking out was confirmed by Mr. Sanchez. There is no question the gal spoke her mind. If she wanted to get money for the school back east, a bank robbery would do the trick."

"Yes, it would, Pat, and convincing naïve boys to help would also make a lot of sense. Let's take the phone back to the office and put one of our people to check for numbers that were called pretty consistently."

"Boss, we also need to check on the two other kids in the botched robbery. They may be as innocent as their Latino buddies, but we had better check. I'll take care of that."

"Good thinking, Pat. They also might be in danger. So, let's put a lookout in front of each of their homes."

CHAPTER 6

A Successful Visit

Dr. Salk greeted Joe Zuma with, "Hello, Detective Zuma, come right in." After Zuma sat down, he looked around and took a deep breath.

"It feels good to be here again, Dr. Salk. I'm not sure what's going on but it feels good to be here."

"What brings you here now?"

"My close colleague Detective Pat Vasquez said that I was humming to myself a lot and I did something with some suspects the other day that was very inappropriate. I started asking them if they knew some songs or Martin Luther King's *I Have a Dream* speech. Pat told me this with Claudia listening and she confirmed that I had been withdrawn lately and had forgotten a few things. She also noticed that I was sleeping more than usual. That's true. I feel like napping every day, even though I have never done it. They asked me to seek help and I agreed. I'm not here just because they asked. I know something must be going on but can't seem to figure out what it is."

"Let's go over all the things that are going on in your life."

"Claudia and I are good. I'm still in love with her and happy to be with her. We are good together as a couple. She has her painting and I have my work. We're both busy but when we see each other, it's very real and connecting. My boys are well. The older one is completing a Ph.D. at UCLA in Computer Engineering and the younger one has a girlfriend and they are about to move in together as he starts graduate school in Davis in Criminology. My work is good and if Pat hadn't said anything that Claudia confirmed, I would have probably continued without coming here."

Dr. Salk waited to see if Zuma would add anything after a minute she spoke.

"Detective Zuma, you did not discuss your relationship with Detective Vasquez. He was always important to you. Is there anything different about it? Is anything going on other than what you have already mentioned?"

Zuma paused. He took a deep breath. He paused again.

"What are you thinking?"

"There's a letter on my desk. I haven't opened it but I know what's in it."

Salk waited.

"A year or so, I had turned down an offer to become the head of the L.A. Police Department. I did it for lots of reasons, all good as far as I was concerned. They asked me if I could recommend someone. I mentioned Pat as a candidate. I forgot about it until a month ago when I was asked to complete a form evaluating Pat. I knew that completing the form meant he had been vetted in every possible way and that I was the last person they needed to approve him and offer him the position that I had turned down.

"And you said it was about a month ago that these lapses at work began: the laughter, humming, and desire for naps."

"And you think there is a connection and you would like me to think if there might be a connection."

Salk waited.

Zuma waited.

"Alright, you're right. Goddamn, I don't want him to leave."

Salk waited.

"I know it will be good for him. I know he will do a goddamn good job. But I will miss him. We work so well together. He gets me. I get him. He's like part of my family."

"Say more about part of your family. Please think of what that might mean."

Zuma paused. He suddenly began sobbing deeply. It was at least two minutes before he could recover and could speak.

"Oh my God. I haven't thought about this since it happened. I told you my wife was killed by a hit-and-run driver. What I forgot is that she was about one month pregnant. I totally forgot about that."

"And might there be a connection to Pats' departure and your lost child?"

"You mean Pat's leaving is like my losing the child?"

"Those are your thoughts, so I assume you feel them to be true."

"I know I was happy when Carol got pregnant because I had always wanted three children."

"So, in a way, Pat is your third child, the one that was killed with Carol, and he is leaving just like the other members of your family are moving forward. Your elder finishing a degree, your younger starting a degree and moving in with a woman. All are moving forward."

"I should be happy that they are all ready to fly."

"You will be, Detective Zuma, but you can also be sad. That is the connection to your depression and lack of sleep. Pat is leaving and you think you are only supposed to be happy for him, but he represents the child you did not have with Carol and the one you did not mourn. You are still in mourning for him, for that lost child, but now, you are but focusing it on Pat. And just because they are all flying away, they still fly back to their homes. And when they come, you will have lots to talk about. And you will enjoy them"

Zuma sat stunned. After a few moments, he smiled and breathed a deep sigh.

"I'll fill out the letter tomorrow and tell Pat and Claudia what is going on. I'm relieved, Dr. Salk. How can I pay you? I brought my checkbook."

"Let me bill you, Detective. Best of luck to you. I know you will enjoy all three of them."

Zuma left the office and started singing to himself.

"One day up near Salinas, I let him slip away. He's looking for that home and I hope he finds it."

It was one of Zuma's favorites and one of the happiest songs he knew because it was about freedom.

Chapter 7

Why Are You Afraid of the Truth?

Pat noticed that when Zuma arrived at work in the morning, he was much cheerier than he had been in a month. He was happy to see his boss that way. He imagined it was because he had been to a therapist but decided it was not his place to ask.

"Boss, we checked the numbers on the phone, and we got the places where Aliya worked and the homes where she tutored. The gal was consistent, and the reports all support each other."

"Say more, Pat."

"The employers canned her because she was telling the cleaning help that they were being paid poorly and they had a right to ask for high wages. The parents of the kids she was working with also said that their nannies were being told they were underpaid and when they asked her to stop doing that, she refused saying something like, 'Why are you afraid of the truth? Are you ashamed of what you are doing? You should be.'"

"That would be a good reason to get her canned. How come she wasn't fired then?"

"Their kids all loved Aliya and the parents felt they could not explain why she would have left. They probably thought she would tell the kids why she was canned and that would have been more embarrassing to them. Now that we know her, I think they were right. Aliya was not the kind of gal who would leave quietly."

"Anything else, Pat, that might help us?"

"Her teachers all described her as very hardworking and ambitious and the one she had hired for singing instruction said she had discussed her plans to go back east to study. When he mentioned the expensive tuition, he said that Aliya simply smiled and said she was not worried about money."

"She sounds like a real special kid, but none of that helps us in this case. I think we're just going to have to wait, Pat. Maybe it was an isolated act that will have no repercussions or impact. We'll see."

He and Pat did not have to wait long. A call came in for a bank robbery that sounded like it could be related to the shootings at the mall.

CHAPTER 8

A Successful Robbery

When Pat and Zuma showed up at the One West Bank on Wilshire at the fourth street, the area had been roped off. The interviews with bank personnel were conducted and the report was that four robbers, wearing face masks, seemed to know exactly what they were doing. They knew how to get cash, disarming the security alarms and cameras, and weren't afraid to speak to each other. They called each other by the names Alpha, Beta, Charlie, and Delta. Alpha seemed to be in charge. One of the security personnel believed Alpha might be a woman. The guard said they knew how to handle their guns. They get away with over $180,000 in cash. When asked about the race of the robbers, all personnel seemed to think they were white but could not be sure because of the face masks which also covered their heads. Bank personnel also felt the robbers were under 25 but could be younger.

"I don't care how young they are, Pat. This is a professional group or a very well-trained group that is just starting out. Let's run a check on any other robberies in California, Nevada, and Arizona that involve masked robbers who travel in a pack of four. This seems far removed from the botched robbery, but something tells me they are related."

CHAPTER 9

A Farewell

Zuma had decided he was not going to tell Pat about the letter from the Los Angeles Police Department Search Committee. He felt the invitation, and Zuma assumed it would be an offer to become head of the department coming from the committee. It might even come from the mayor.

"Boss, we need to talk. I just got this letter from the Mayor or Los Angeles. Can you believe it? It was addressed to me personally."

Zuma held his breath.

"They want me to become head of the whole bloody department. You must have had something to do with this. Are you trying to get rid of me?"

Zuma laughed. "No, Pat, they want you."

"How can I go, Boss? We work so well together, we're buddies. I don't want to leave."

"Sure, you don't want to leave. We do work very well, we are buddies, and you're like family to me. I also don't want you to leave, but you are going to leave. You must leave. It will be good for you and the city of Los Angeles and we may end up working together on cases. When do you start?"

"They wanted to hear from me within 48 hours, but I can start right away if I want to or any time within a month. I want to finish up this case."

"Pat, start whenever it is best for you. I can handle this case without you."

"Ok, I'll think about it. Since I'm going to leave, I need to check something with you. I really hit it off with one of the teachers who worked with Aliya. I told her I could not see her until the case was closed. Since I'm off the case, would it be cool to date her?"

Zuma smiled. Dr. Salk was right. It was like his son ready to move out into the world.

"Pat, it probably is legal, but you might want to play it safe. You are going to be under a microscope from the press. They will investigate everything about you. You're entering a new game with all kinds of new rules. If they find out you're dating someone who you met on a case, even though you're off the case, it has not been solved. It wouldn't be fair to the woman either."

"You see, Boss, that's why I don't want to leave. How am I going to figure things like that out?"

"You will, Pat. You will. And you can always call home. But since you are still working here, let's get down to business and see what we've got. Put it up on the drawing board."

CHAPTER 10

Clues

"Boss, this is what we got. Two robberies, one botched by four kids, two of whom get shot later. No suspects. The other robbery is successful, three of whom were considered male and the fourth a possible female, all thought to be under 25, and who could be white. No suspects. Just wise guy names and one gal with a motive to make money who has a history for an armed robbery attempt with a non-guilty verdict."

"How could young kids be so sophisticated? Maybe there was an inside person in the bank or maybe someone is training kids to steal so they can supply money to someone who would pay for drugs. Convincing kids to do armed robbery is easier to do with kids. It's more exciting than buying and selling the drugs and they will be instructed on the lesser penalties for a first offense."

"I don't think it's going to stop with this one successful job, Boss."

"I'm sure you're right, Pat."

The detectives did not have to wait long. Another robbery took place at a different One West Bank, on twelfth and Wilshire. The same MO was used: face and head masks and speaking together. This time, it was Echo, Foxtrot, Golf, and Hotel.

"Pat, it has to be more than a coincidence that they are using these military names to speak to each other. Maybe the trainer is a veteran? Can we check with the Veterans Administration in West L.A. and see who has been released from service in the past 12 months? Look especially for dishonorable discharges, someone from an intelligence unit, or who had sharpshooting skills. This is our first warm clue."

"Boss, it can't be just a coincidence that the same branch of the bank was robbed."

"Pat, that's our second warm clue. Let's find out if the banks have any veterans that are working there."

Pat knew that Zuma was excited as he was because the toothpick had come out of Zuma's shirt pocket and Zuma was humming the Dylan song "Blowin' in the Wind."

The search for discharged veterans revealed over a hundred in number but the search narrowed when the bank reported they had two veterans working at each of the two banks.

"Pat, we don't want to alert these guys if they are the brains behind the operation. We need to interview all employees. We'll bring in a crew and you and I will make sure we do the vets. You take the first bank and bring in two other officers. I'll take the second and bring in the same number. Let's make sure we find out what outfits they served in. Maybe two of them were together and hatched this operation. When we interview, we need to find out from all employees where they were, and can they account for their time when the shootings at the mall occurred? We frame it as a question that we just need to follow up on. We say we don't think there is any connection, but we are just exploring it as a possibility. Let's check back later after we do the interviews."

"What did you find, Pat?"

"All six employees say they were not at the mall at the time of the shooting and can account for their whereabouts. Both of the vets were giving brief answers. I don't think they were suspicious. They're just military guys. I got the units they served in. One was overseas in Iraq and the other stateside."

"Pat, I think we got a bingo. One of the vets I interviewed also served in Iraq."

"What's our next step?"

"We're going to have to put a tail on each one. Pick your sharpest people, Pat. They're military and used at observing details. It may take some time. If they communicate with their gang of kids as they have to meet with them sometime to collect money. We're just going to have to be patient. Let's go to dinner tonight and you can tell Claudia about your good news."

"There's too much good news, Boss: warm clues, possible lady, and a new job."

"I know you can handle it, Pat, and you'd better get used to it."

CHAPTER 11

A Booking

Three days after the last robbery, a youngish white male showed up at the home of one of the vets. After about ten minutes, the young man left and Solomon Johnson came out carrying a brown paper bag. They tailed him and he went directly to the VA in Westwood. The tails called Zuma. They thought something important was going to happen. When Zuma and Pat showed up, there were a lot of vets basking in the sun and schmoozing.

Someone who Zuma did not recognize was approaching the vets. As soon as they saw this man approaching, they began to line up as if they were still a company in the military. The vets in wheelchairs and walkers were in the front. When the man got closer, they all smiled. He saluted them and they saluted him in return. Before we get started, I think we should have a bit of a concert. Some of the vets started chanting "Johnny, Johnny." One of them got up with a guitar and went to the front.

"Hi, I'm Johnny. Not Johnny Cash. No, I have no cash. I'm like all of you and we are all busted. When you see me here, you can call me Johnny Busted." He starts to sing.

> My bills are all due and the baby needs shoes and I'm busted
> Cotton is down to a quarter a pound, but I'm busted
> I got a cow that went dry and a hen that won't lay

A big stack of bills that gets bigger each day
The county's gonna haul my belongings away 'cause I'm busted
I went to my brother to ask for a loan 'cause I was busted
I hate to beg like a dog without his bone, but I'm busted
My brother said there ain't a thing I can do
My wife and my kids are all down with the flu
And I was just thinking about calling on you and I'm busted
Well, I am no thief, but a man can go wrong when he's…
Well, I am no thief, but a man can go wrong when he's busted
The food that we canned last summer is gone and I'm busted
The fields are all bare and the cotton won't grow
Me and my family got to pack up and go
But I'll make a living, just where I don't know 'cause I'm busted
I'm broke, no bread, I mean like nothing

"Thank you, Johnny. Company V, you have all made the ultimate sacrifice for your country. You no longer can have the lives you were once hoping to have. I am grateful. Perhaps someday, the government and the Veteran's Administration will be able to genuinely honor you. In the meantime, I honor you with this small payment for the service you have rendered and the lives you can no longer have."

The stranger proceeded to distribute bills until the bag was empty. The Zuma saw that each vet was handed three $100 bills. Zuma counted thirty-one vets. The stranger saluted them, they saluted back, and he left.

"That was quite a concert, Boss. It's a song that Cash sang when he was singing to the inmates at Folsom Prison. I think our vets identify with those inmates, lacking freedom and busted. Cash always sang about the underdogs, how they were treated, and the hard times they had. I think you will love many of his songs. His messages are universal even though he came from a tiny town in Arkansas called Dyess."

"Getting back to our problems, Boss, why would someone train kids to rob banks and get money which he would then give away?"

"Someone who has a lot of feelings about veterans. Someone who doesn't care much about money. Someone who might be angry at the government, the VA, or the armed services."

"But why wouldn't they do it themselves? Why use kids?"

"If they got caught, the distribution would end. This is a way to put someone between themselves and possible detection. They probably carefully selected kids with clean records so if the kids did get caught, the courts would not be hard on them."

"And what about the mall shootings, Boss?"

"I don't know yet."

"What do we do now?"

"We can pick up the guy who delivered the money or the kid who delivered the cash. The guy who we don't know yet is a vet. He will give us nothing. They're trained to give nothing. I'm sure we'll have better luck with the kid. Let's keep a trail on him. If the $180,000 was divided up between the kids, the vet, and Solomon, that still leaves $90,000. I calculate he gave a little over $9,000 out at the VA. There's a lot left over. We have to find out what else might be going on with the cash. Even if they do nothing, that allows for ten months of trips to the VA."

"Young man, the name on the doorbell doesn't match your other name. Was it Alpha or Charlie? Or were you Foxtrot?"

Alex Maxwell smiled.

"Am I being charged with anything? If so, I need to call my lawyer."

"You could save yourself a lot of trouble by telling us what was in the bag you delivered to Mr. Solomon Johnson."

"What bag?"

"Ok, Mr. Maxwell, or Foxtrot, or whatever you like to be called, we're taking you in and we'll be booking you on a charge of aiding and abetting an armed robbery. Here's my phone. Call your lawyer now."

Everyone in the room knew that there was no proof of what was in the bag. The best that Zuma could hope for was to keep the young man overnight while he searched for the other kid. The lawyer pointed out the spotless record of the young man. Zuma approached the judge and pointed out that the man who received the bag, whatever was in it, was involved in a case of other armed robberies and he would like some time. The judge complied telling the defense attorney that he looks upon armed bank robberies as a serious offense.

"I'll give you 48 hours. If nothing comes up, Mr. Maxwell will be released."

"Where does that leave us, Boss?"

"I'm not sure, Pat. Solomon is not going to budge and contact the others. Maybe the other kids will get antsy when they don't hear from or see their buddy and do something silly or stupid."

Zuma and Pat did not have to wait long. Another but different One West Bank robbery on 16th and Montana occurred, with the same MO. This time, the names were India, Juliet, Kilo, and Lima.

"I guess they were not stupid, Boss. They pulled it off and they got another replacement. That's going to make it impossible to keep Maxwell locked up."

"Not only that. How did they replace him? How were they able to act so quickly? This must have been in their plans."

"We're back to where we were. We have to wait and see if they drop off money. I think it will be a while. Solomon might not be able to wait. Let's make sure we have a 24/7 watch on both of them. Let's pick up Mr. Be Kind to Veterans and see what we can find out. I don't think much, and I know he knows we're watching him but let's put a face on this operation."

CHAPTER 12

Where Have All the Flowers Gone?

"Pat, we got a break. A kid just walked into a One West Bank and opened up an account for $25,000. All the tellers have been wary after the robbery, but the kid must have thought since it was a different branch from the ones that were robbed, that he would be ok. He may not have even known about the other robberies. It must have been that fresh recruit. The bank manager called and gave us his name and address."

The name on the doorbell was Paul and the knock on the door was responded to by a young man.

"I'm not sure what you would like to be called. We can use names you're accustomed to such as Kilo or Lima. Do your parents use that name?"

The young man was speechless. It was obvious to Pat and Zuma that this was a raw recruit.

"Peter, who are you talking to? Don't be rude and make them stand there. Invite them in."

The boy nodded and the detectives entered. The woman was surprised to see the uniforms.

"What's going on, detectives? Is something wrong? Is my son in trouble?"

"We are not sure, Mrs. Paul. Your son made a very large deposit in a bank and Detective Vasquez and I would like to know where he got this sum of money. There have been a number of bank robberies recently, and we thought Peter might know something about them as well as help us understand where he obtained the cash he deposited."

"Peter, what is going on? I told you to stop hanging out with Jack and the other three kids that seemed like they were a gang. Where did you get all that money from?"

The son clammed up and just stood there.

"Talk to these gentlemen, Peter. You'll be better off talking than just standing there. If you're in trouble, Dad and I will help but you've got to cooperate with these gentlemen. And I want to know the truth."

"Mom, I can't give names. They will get even. I'll lose the few friends I have. I'll just say what I did. Here it goes. I was asked to join this group. They didn't tell me what they were going to do. They showed me a gun, gave me a face mask, and gave me a name.

They said I would never have to shoot it. It seemed like it could be fun. All I had to do was go along with them and I would be given $25,000. It seemed really easy and that I could earn so much money was unbelievable to me."

"Mrs. Park, we are going to take your son and book him for armed robbery. I suggest you get a lawyer. Before we leave, Mrs. Park, if you don't mind, I'd like to ask you a question. Would your first name, by any chance, be Mary?"

"Detective, you are also obviously a fan like my husband and I are. When we got married, we decided that if we were to have a son, we would name him Peter. We attended as many concerts as we could. Our favorite was 'Where Have All the Flowers Gone?'"

On the way back to the jail to book Peter Park, Pat inquired about the guess that Zuma had made to Mrs. Park.

"Ok, Boss, tell me about that group. You never referred to them before."

"They picked up the legacy of Woody Guthrie with their social commentary about the war. They started in the sixties but performed well into the 70s. They are probably best known for a children's song 'Puff the Magic Dragon.'"

"Boss, I know that one. They taught it to us in public school."

On the way to the booking, Pat received a phone call.

"That was the mayor. He wants me to start tomorrow. It seems there has been a bit of a crime wave and he feels he needs to do something to assure the public. I wanted to check with you, Boss."

"First of all, Pat, you don't say no to the mayor. I can take it from here. I'll be fine and so will you. Secondly, you've got to stop calling me Boss. Joe will be just fine."

"Sure, Boss." Zuma roared with laughter. Pat was happy to see his boss laughing.

CHAPTER 13

Another Bank

The entire Park family along with the lawyer were at the booking. The lawyer and the parents had asked for a moment where they could talk to Peter. When they were alone with him, they tried to get Peter to cooperate and give the names of his accomplices pointing out that his buddies were probably already upset at him for doing something stupid. They were not going to be friends as they could no longer trust him. He had nothing to lose and could gain by being cooperative. The lawyer reassured the family that because of Peter's clean record and his cooperation, he was not likely to receive a harsh sentence.

While waiting for the hearing for Peter, the three accomplices were picked up.

As each one of the three was picked up, they called the same lawyer who arrived at the jail shortly after the boys arrived.

"Detective Zuma, you have no basis for booking these three young men. They have and will testify that at the time of the robberies, they were playing basketball at Santa Monica City College. Do you have any other charges?"

"We have the sworn testimony of someone who was with them at the time of the robbery."

"Obviously, it's the testimony of some disgruntled young men wanting to seek revenge for something totally unrelated to the robbery or perhaps in exchange for his having committed some crime."

Zuma knew he had no case. His only hope for a conviction was to show that the boys had suddenly acquired or spent lots of money. He felt defeated and admitted that he was missing Pat. After deciding not to book the boys, he drove back to the precinct.

The officers had the TV on and were watching the mayor introducing Pat Vasquez as the new Chief of Police for the City of Los Angeles. He smiled and felt proud. It was similar to a feeling he had when his son had been admitted to the UCLA doctoral program in computer engineering.

He hoped that he could get warrants to get into the boys' homes and look for cash or check to see if they had made deposits in banks, probably different from One West. He told the officer who had been next in line for Pat's position of working directly with Zuma to prepare the paperwork so they could get warrants to search three homes.

"Officer Granger, remember we will need three separate warrants."

"Boss, it looks like we'll still be working together. I have two murders on my plate but that's not why I'm calling. A bank called the Hab was robbed. Same MO, military names, starting with Alpha. Bank was downtown on Broadway. They were just moving there from another location close by. Someone had to be in on the whole move."

"Pat, I guess you'll do what we did before. Let's find out if there are any vets working at Hab and check their unit. This network may be bigger than we thought. Is there a way to see if anyone at Hab was communicating with anyone at One West?"

"I'll get back to you, Boss."

"Pat, are you forgetting? I'm no longer your boss. Claudia and my kids call me Joe and that's what I'd like you to do. Please remember to do that."

"I will, Boss."

Zuma roared with laughter.

CHAPTER 14

Buddies

"Joe, there was another vet working at the Hab bank. He was from the same military outfit that Aliya's father was in. How do you want to work on this? Shall I bring him in separately from your bringing in Aliya's dad?"

"Yes, Pat, let's see if they know each other."

Neither Solomon nor Juseph Jackson indicated knowledge of the other. Zuma knew this to be untrue since Juseph had been handing out the money at the VA. When confronted with the phone calls that had been made, they acknowledged they had been in Afghanistan together.

"Solomon, did you fight side by side with Juseph?"

"We did. He was always looking out for me and me for him. We were lucky to get out alive and unhurt. We knew we were going to be friends for the rest of our lives."

"Does he know your wife and daughter?"

"He has met them."

"So, when you chat now, what do you talk about? Do you have any business plans that you're both involved in?"

"No plans, just two army buddies sharing gossip about other vets and how our families are doing. I have answered a lot of questions, Detective. Now, can you answer my question about progress in finding out who shot my daughter?"

"Nothing yet, Mr. Johnson."

When Pat called to tell what he found out from Juseph, it matched what Solomon had told Zuma.

"Pat, I'm going to do a search of the three kids who were picked up. I also think I need to account for Aliya's whereabouts at the time of the Hab bank robbery. Can you put a tap on the calls that Juseph makes to Solomon?" You'll need to get permission from the manager."

"That won't be a problem, Joe. I'm sure he wants this crime solved and if possible, the money returned. I'll wait to hear from you and hopefully, you'll find money in the kid's homes."

The search of the young men's three homes found no money, but bank books, which were kept in the kids' desks, revealed that each had made deposits for one-fourth of the money that was stolen. The kids all had the same cover story about winning the money in a crap game. Zuma knew that was a load of crap and there was still a lot of money to be accounted for.

He calculated that there were five possible suspects. Aliya could have been on the robberies. Solomon and Juseph might have a part in the planning and training of the kids and the two vets from the One West Bank. All of them could have shot the two Latino boys. He would have to get warrants for locating bank statements for all five suspects. He knew this would not be a problem for a judge.

Chapter 15

All Decent Chaps

When the tail on Solomon told that he was with Juseph in a restaurant, Zuma decided to show up.

"Detective, please join us. We were just sharing old war stories about ourselves, our buddies, and our philanthropy. Let us treat you to dinner and stories."

"Thanks, gentlemen, for the offer of dinner. I'm quite interested in your philanthropy. Is this something new?"

"The idea started when we're still in combat. We saw and heard how hard it was for our returning buddies to get decent and quick help from the Veterans Administration. We decided when we got back, we would raise money for a fund so that any vet who applied would be able to get money quickly without questions. We had a great response from all over the country from citizens and veterans."

"Who handles the deposits and the requests?"

"Aliya was doing it in the beginning She is very tech-savvy, but it's growing and getting too big even for her. We were just trying to figure out who else we could get to handle this. Neither of us is that good with computers."

"You could hire someone from the banks you are associated with. You have a couple of vets in your bank, Solomon. Would they be interested?"

"Good suggestion, Detective. We'll think about who might be best for the job."

Zuma felt very comfortable talking with these two men. Maybe it was because they were direct and military-like, like him, or that they were very decent chaps. He forgot for a moment that they were suspects in a series of robberies and possible murders. He was stuck again with the way both of the men's boots were polished, even though one wore black and the other wore brown boots.

"Continue success with your fundraising efforts, gentlemen. I enjoyed hearing about it."

"Feel free to contribute, Detective. Here's our card so that you can ask your friends to help out. There is no overhead. All the time is donated, and money goes directly to the vets for surgeries, prosthetics, and medications."

"I'll have to wait to contribute until these cases of robberies and shootings are solved."

When Zuma left, he wondered how Aliya could be giving so much time to the work. Maybe there was skimming involved. How could he find out? Would it even be illegal? After all, they could claim she was on salary. There had to be some records filed with the state or feds about their philanthropy. He would ask his new assistant to pursue this. He also knew this information would probably not shed any light on the crimes he was trying to solve.

CHAPTER 16

The Student Reminds the Mentor

"Joe, do you recall I said there were two murders on my plate? We traced the guys down with their fingerprints. They were both vets and believe it or not, one worked in the first bank that was robbed in Santa Monica and the other worked at the Hab. They're awaiting trial now. They raised a lot of bail money. Each of them was involved in separate shootings but both were downtown putting them in my precinct. I think this means we can work together. Also, some witnesses said one of the shooters wore a ski mask, and they were not sure if it was a male or a female."

"It does, Pat. You work your Hab guy and find out what his phone records and bank statements reveal. I'll work on the Santa Monica side of the case. Let's connect as soon as we get all these records."

"Sure, Joe."

The lack of clarity regarding the male-female identity of the shooter made Zuma feel it was more likely to be a female. A male would have more difficulty acting female than a female acting male. He began thinking of a strong woman and Aliya kept coming up in his mind.

"Joe, we found quite a bit of money in one of the vets' accounts. He had put it in another bank. Seemed like there were regular monthly deposits."

"Ditto on that, Pat. They were working together. If they were skimming a lot from each of their banks, they would have been detected. They must have used the money for something else. The only thing that small amounts of cash would generate is drugs which could be sold."

"They might have used someone to buy the drugs and sell. Or maybe it was more than one person buying."

"Also, Pat, maybe this was a separate operation from the other crimes. Maybe they were each operating unbeknownst to each other."

"But their murders can't be isolated from the other events. Joe, you were the one who taught me there are no coincidences when it comes to murder."

Zuma liked that Pat had remembered what he had taught him and was reminding Zuma of his mentoring.

"Let's keep someone posted at each of the victims' homes. Even if they're dead, someone might show up to collect or to give money. We should also interview the members of their families. I assume both of them had wives.

Vets usually do.

CHAPTER 17

An innocent Helps

The interviews with each of the wives revealed the same story. Their husbands had kept the business affairs of the family to themselves. The women had wondered where the extra money was coming from, but they figured it was because their husbands were working late for a few nights a week. The kids were just happy to have some extra spending allowance.

The officer on duty at the home of one of the victims saw a young man standing at the front door of the suspects' home screaming.

"I've got to have the money. They will think I stole it. They will never believe me. It wasn't under the bushes. He must have left it with you. You have it. I know you have it."

When the young man was approached, he insisted he had done nothing and there was no reason to be detained.

"You're creating a nuisance and I'm taking you downtown."

Pat saw the young man was very unsophisticated. He hadn't asked for a lawyer.

"I'll be happy to overlook this, so you won't have anything on your record, but you have to tell us everything you know."

"Some guy, I don't even know his name, picked me up as I was walking home from school and said I could make $200 a week by running two errands to two different addresses. I would just deliver something and pick up something. The pick-ups were at the side of the house. I never met anyone in the house. I was never to look into the bag. It seemed so simple. What kid wouldn't want to earn two hundred a week for just more than two hours of work?"

"How long had you been doing this?"

"About 6 months."

"So, you have made close to five grand. Is that correct? What are you planning to do with the money?"

"I was hoping to get a car when I was 19."

"We might be able to let you keep the money. We will try and do that, but this is what you have to do. Tell us the size of the bag. We're going to put money in there and you are going to drop it off. You'll be off the hook for stealing cash. It will never be known that you showed us where the folks collecting the cash lived."

The home where the cash was delivered was known to the drug enforcement program of Pats' precinct. It had been under surveillance for a while, but nothing had been uncovered. This was the break everyone had been looking for. Pat and two other officers from drug enforcement waited two hours after the cash had been delivered before they knocked on the door with their emergency warrant to inspect the home of Alvin Duplex.

Mr. Duplex looked the warrant over carefully and said he wanted to place a phone call to his lawyer.

"And what am I being charged with, officers?"

"Right now, it's only suspicion of selling and buying drugs. I'm sure more will be uncovered, especially your unpaid income taxes on all the unreported income you have been making."

Pat called Zuma while Duplex was being driven to the precinct downtown.

"The vets were loaning money to a dealer who would buy drugs, sell, and pay back the vets. That doesn't help with the murders, but Joe, we landed a big-time dealer."

"Always good to hear about one less dealer put out of business. You're right about this not necessarily helping with the murders. But we shall see. Let's each of us put our thinking hats on."

CHAPTER 18

Another Alpha

Aliya had been on the books of the philanthropies for expenses totaling $50,000 a year. Zuma knew it would be a waste of time to pursue this. She was on her way back east to a program in the performing arts. It had to be one of the Afghan vets. Solomon and his wife were the only other possible suspects for the murders. His thinking was not helping. He knew he would have to go back to the beginning. He decided to speak with his new aid as he had always done with Pat.

"Zack, let's assume they were innocents who botched the job. But why would two of those innocents be killed? What would the motive be for that?"

"Maybe it was a warning to others about robbing One West Banks. The kid's pictures were in the papers so they could be identified. They just happened to be in the wrong place. Maybe the black kids would have been shot if they had been on the mall?"

"Good thinking. If we follow that line of reasoning, it would mean that someone in or out of the bank was trying to present closer scrutiny of bank practices or employees which we have already done. We need to go back and check the employees. There were two vets who did not seem to have any connection to the Afghan vets and who seemed squeaky clean. Can you get on that and pursue them more carefully? Bank records would be valuable. I'll go back and talk with Solomon and his wife."

Solomon repeated that Aliya's money went to the philanthropy and that he and his wife were at home at the time of the shooting in the mall. Zuma knew it was an airtight alibi.

"We are a team, Detective Zuma. Solomon is an alpha but so am I."

The last comment from Solomon's wife struck Zuma over the head. It was an alpha type of female who was in on the robberies. He decided to say nothing and would figure out how and why she had been involved.

This time, the investigation of the two other vets from One West proved more fruitful. Zack had widened the search to out-of-state deposits and found regular monthly deposits for an amount of $100 a month to each of the two accounts. This had been going on for a year. He and Zuma decided they would call each of them in separately. They had obviously prepared a cover story. Each reported that they worked together at night to help other banks with their problems. They were paid by checks and these were deposited. They both agreed they were trying to avoid state taxes.

"We could if we decided to report this to your employers. I'm sure they would fire you. Is there something else you can tell us about this money? What were you planning to use it for?"

"Nothing special. We were hoping to use this in our retirement. We don't make a lot of money working in the bank. It did not seem fair since we had been willing to put our lives on the line. The other tellers had risked nothing. We had."

Zuma decided to make an offer.

"Give the money back to the bank. I will seek to get them to not press charges or fire you. I'll also speak to them about a raise because of your veterans' status."

"Thank you, Officer Zuma. We appreciate your recognition of our service to this country."

CHAPTER 19

Working with the Enemy

Alvin Duplex and his lawyer were extremely calm. Zuma and Pat recognized that it was a high-priced law firm from downtown that specialized in criminal law and by definition, made it more difficult to get guilty charges.

"What are the charges, Detective?"

"We have no evidence that your client was involved with the selling of drugs, but he has received money, so we suspect he has been getting money from dealers and hides it from the Feds. He, in return, takes his percentage and also hides it from the Feds. We are going to do a search of all his accounts in the US."

"That will get you nothing, detectives. And I'm sure you know why."

With these last words, Alvin Duplex dropped his head. Zuma caught the look. Duplex turned to Zuma and indicated he needed to speak privately to his lawyer.

"I may have screwed things up by making made a large deposit to a US bank. I couldn't get into my offshore account, but I didn't want to keep it around the house."

"How much did you deposit?"

"$350,000."

"That's too much. The Feds will want to investigate. They'll believe if you made that large a deposit, you must be hiding your source of funds."

"I know that. What I'm thinking is that I tell them about a few of the offshores. I keep most of them secret. I'll agree to turn the money to them and pay taxes on all of it in exchange for not going to jail."

"It's a risky offer. I'd advise against it. But it is probably the best chance you have for not doing jail time. Shall I make the offer, or will you?"

Zuma listed carefully while Duplex spoke. After he finished, Pat Vasquez spoke.

"We are willing to go to the judge with the information you gave us but I want something else from you before I do that."

"And what is that?"

"I want all the names of the dealers who asked you to hide their money. And I want your help in a murder investigation."

Duplex thought about Pats' request. If he were to give up only three dealers, the larger number would not be caught, and he would probably not become a target. He liked the idea that he was being asked to help with a murder investigation instead of being accused.

"We have a deal. Here are the names. You go to the judge and present my case and just tell me when I start working with you."

CHAPTER 20

Cooperation Doesn't Pay

"Joe, what's your thinking about getting Duplex to help us?"

"I think we ask him to make large deposits twice a week in one of the One West Banks that Solomon and Juseph are familiar with. He will probably come to their attention. It would seem likely that they will approach him hoping for a donation. After Duplex agrees to a donation, he can put out a proposition to help them make lots of money. If they turn him down, we have lost nothing. If they buy in, we can put a wire on both of them and arrest one or the other because they have become involved in investing money with a known drug dealer. Even if they say they did not know who he was, we can possibly use that against them to get more information about bank robberies and murders."

When Solomon Johnson approached Alvin Duplex, he was most appreciative of the philanthropy that Solomon was running and indicated his respect to Solomon by saying he was doing what the government should be doing and offered $1500.00 as a contribution. But when Duplex broached the possibility of making a large return on an operation that he, Duplex, were to run, Solomon was also appreciative but rejected the offer.

"I've given you the names you asked for, Detective. I have complied with your request to speak to Solomon Johnson and I expect you to keep your end of our agreement by informing the judge about my cooperativeness."

"You had our word. We are good for that."

Zuma decided he had to go back and check Solomon again. There were so few suspects, but he seemed the more likely of the bunch. It was the day that Solomon and Juseph were going to be at the VA and Zuma decided to again watch the ceremony of payment to the vets and speak with Solomon after it was over.

While he was waiting for the noon hour, a call came in from Pat that Alvin Duplex had been murdered while he was coming out of his home.

"Pat, any witnesses? What do you have?"

"Pretty much nothing. The person was a good shooter. It was a clean shot right to the heart. Must have been from across the street because one witness who heard the shot came out of his home and saw a car speeding away but could not be sure what model it was. Just said it was black."

"I guess he paid the price for cooperating. Poor bastard might have been better off just going to jail for tax evasion. Pat, I'm on my way to see the ceremony at the VA. Do whatever else needs to be done with the crime scene, the body, and next of kin, if any. Let's check-in later and talk. Make sure his lawyers know and find out what is going to happen with all the offshore accounts of his. I'm going to speak to Solomon Johnson after the ceremony."

"Solomon, you are lucky to have gotten a contribution from Mr. Duplex. It was probably one of his last acts. He was murdered this morning."

"I knew he was a shady character and that you know about it makes me realize you were behind it."

"So, what do you want, Detective? You keep bugging me. What more can I tell you? When are you going to stop?"

"I will cease my bugging you as soon as we can find out the murderer or murderers. Can you give me any clues?"

"You've got to be kidding me. You send a guy to trap me who was cooperating with you and look what happened to him. You want me to cooperate? If I could, I would, but I can't." And with this last comment, Solomon Johnson walked away.

CHAPTER 21

Going back

"Joe, Alvin Duplex had no family. The lawyers said the accounts would be frozen. They were going to find out whether the Feds would be able to get the money or the offshore banks could keep it."

"Did they think the folks he was hiding money from would be able to get their money back?"

"They said they would be very unlikely since it would expose them to declaring income and they would be worried about tax evasion charges. Where do we go from here, Joe?"

"I don't know, Pat. I think the shooter of the two Latino kids is key. It was someone who is a good shot and the fact that a female-like person was involved in the robberies makes me think the shooter might be the same female. I need to think. If you come up with any ideas, give me a call. Let's plan to talk in a day or so. I think you and I are going to go back again to the Johnsons."

"I'll be ready, Joe. Why do we have to wait a day? The lawyers on the Duplex case have nothing to add to our efforts to solve the murders. I think we should do it today."

"You're right, Pat. Let's meet there at four."

Joe Zuma liked that Pat was showing his independence by making a suggestion the case that was different than his.

As Zuma and Pat were getting ready to knock on the door of the Johnsons, they heard a loud conversation between the couple. They decided to listen in.

"Solomon, you know I love you, so let me confess to this. I have a great war record. I could always plead PTSD and I don't think the court would be too harsh on me since I'm a woman. You go find the very best lawyer who has done well for vets. We can afford it even if we have to fly him in from the east coast."

"I don't want you to confess. Let me do it."

"Solomon, I can also confess to the robberies and indicate why I shot the Latino kids. They are more likely to be easier on me if they solve the robberies and get their murderer. This way, you can continue to do well with the philanthropy."

The Johnsons opened the door when they heard the knocking and allowed the detectives to enter.

"We overheard your conversations about confessing and we thought we should alert the two of you to some new information. The parents and the families of the Latino kids who were shot have set up a reward of $250,000 for the killers of their children. They are also seeking to have the district attorney pursue the issue as a hate crime."

"Thank you, Detective, but I don't see what that has to do with us."

"Well, if you confess to something that you haven't done and are let off, it could be the start of a race war in this city. I can already see the headline: 'Interracial couple is set free and murder of Latinos still unsolved.' I don't want that to happen and I'm trying to prevent it.

If you have any information that could help, I am asking you again for help. If that is all you have to say to us, we can say goodbye now."

As the detectives were leaving, they overheard Adar speak.

"Solomon, I think we can change our plans."

After another minute making sure the detectives had left, Adar spoke.

"Let's get Juseph to turn me in. He can collect the reward and use it for the philanthropy. He will refuse but you will tell him what our arrangement was and that I was planning to confess."

"My brilliant Alpha, Adar my darling, you're a genius. I need to look for a lawyer right after I speak to Juseph. My genius wife deserves a genius lawyer."

CHAPTER 22

The Trial

Juseph agreed to point out the suspect once he understood what the arrangement was. He had to make up a story of how he knew about the murder without implicating Solomon. They both decided that Juseph heard it from a vet who had been at the mall when the shooting occurred. The vet had told him at the ceremony. He said that the vet was no longer coming around to the ceremonies and even if he did, he could not be sure he could identify him. The story worked. Juseph collected the reward money. Adar was arrested and the Latino families felt good that they had contributed to the capture of their children's murderer. Solomon found a 'genius' lawyer in California who had successfully pleaded a great number of PTSD cases.

The trial drew a lot of publicity. The prosecution sought to indict Adar because of her jealousy of Latinos, her anger about the treatment her husband had received as a black war hero, and the ways in which Moslems were treated. The lawyer argued that the name Adar, in Arabic, meant fire and this woman was a fire ready to hurt people. Zuma saw that the prosecution was seeking to recreate the stereotype of the angry, revenge-seeking Muslim, and did not like it even though he knew the woman was guilty. Adar sat quietly in her dress of blue marine outfit with polished black boots. There were other vets in the courtroom. The dark blue Marine dress uniforms and the dark green Army outfits along with the shining shoes make the courtroom sparkle. It looked to everyone to be like a pageant. The judge had never seen such a display of color and liked it and decided he would like to walk into his courtroom with something besides gray-painted walls

The defense kept taking the wind out of the prosecution's argument by agreeing that Adar was angry but had a good reason to be.

"The treatment by the VA of Solomon's wounds was a very personal thing. What good wife would not be angry? She is a decorated war veteran and an American heroine."

"Mrs. Johnson, will you now please speak?"

"I know how to control my anger at the enemy for losing my comrades on the battlefield but as a citizen, this treatment by my government to the VA and other citizens has been too much. It was not what I was expecting after risking my life to defend yours and my country."

Zuma thought Mrs. Johnson's last argument would probably be the one that gets to the jurors. It made them come face to face with a person who had sacrificed and risked her life for them. Zuma thought that most of them might feel guilty that they had not served. He thought 'sometimes guilt is a good thing.'

The defense spoke, "Ladies and gentlemen of the jury, if you had risked your life and had seen your husband risk his life and returned to a country, would you not each and every one of you have expected some respect and excellent treatment from the government? If your answer to yourself is "yes," you will be most lenient on my client who has fought for us all and bring in a verdict of not guilty or guilty with special circumstances which will allow the judge to make a decision about a penalty."

When Adar got up to leave and to await the judicial decision, a number of vets in the courtroom, many of them marines, stood up, saluted her, and shouted Semper Fi and Oorah. Zuma knew this to be the greeting that Marines often gave to each other indicating enthusiasm to see the other.

It took a few days before a verdict was delivered. The Latino community picketed the court with signs asking for justice for Latinos, and vets picketed the court with signs saying justice for vets and better treatment for vets.

There was a trio of musicians that kept playing the Marine hymn as a way of showing their loyalty to Adar.

There was no antagonism since a number of vets were Latinos so there would be no race war regardless of the outcome.

The jury came back with a verdict of guilty with special circumstances allowing the judge to decide on the penalty. He thanked the jurors, informed that they were not permitted to discuss what had gone on in the juror's room, and told the waiting press outside that he would render a decision in a few days.

Outside the apartment where the Johnsons lived, a bugler came every night to blow taps. The neighbors started coming out and talking with each other and to the Johnsons. Solomon Johnson was finally getting the respect from his fellow countrymen that he had wanted.

At the precinct, Zack asked if this was an easy or hard case. He said it seemed easy because Adar had confessed.

"No case is ever easy, Zack. They're all unique and different. I actually found this one harder than a lot of others I have solved or worked on. It may not even be over. If that vet turns up that Juseph spoke about, it might reveal they were all in on it and were all guilty. That would complicate the case. If Solomon's philanthropy is investigated and they begin to question Aliya's salary, it may cause him to do something. Sometimes, a case only seems like it has ended. Please excuse me now. I am heading to dinner. You're going to make a fine, Detective."

The judge put Adar on parole for two years and made her pay a fine of $5,000 and do service in the Latino community.

Pat brought his lady friend to dinner with Zuma and Claudia. The woman was black, and her name was Keisha. Zuma stood up to make a toast. As he stood there, the words to the Randy Newman song 'You've Got a Friend in Me" played in his head.

> "And as the years go by,
> Our friendship will never die
> You're gonna see it's our destiny
> You've got a friend in me."

"I want to celebrate the solving of our case, to the improving race relations in our country, to our new friend Keisha, and to each of us who are fortunate enough to know each other. May it continue."

The sound of taps came through the pane glass window of the Shangri-La. They all looked. A marine dressed in the dark blue Marine Corp uniform was blowing his bugle while the rain was coming down with Adar holding an umbrella over his head. Claudia spoke, "Joe, the Johnsons know how much you respected them, and this is the best way they know of saying thank you and showing their respect for you. I'm sure it was hard for them. You were and are a cop."

The party sat and gazed at the bugler. When he finished playing, he saluted them, turned around sharply, and marched off into the night.

The end.

www.ingramcontent.com/pod-product-compliance
Lightning Source LLC
Chambersburg PA
CBHW021451070526
44577CB00002B/362